Rachel Blau DuPlessis

DRAFTS
3-14

Rachel Blau DuPlessis

Potes & Poets Press, Elmwood Connecticut • 1991

Typesetting, Ruth Boerger and Marc Erdrich, Roxbury, CT
Printing, Thomson-Shore, Dexter, MI
Cover design, Rachel Blau DuPlessis,
    prepared by Avid, Inc., Hartford, CT

This book has been partially funded by the National Endowment
for the Arts, a Federal agency.
ISBN 0-937013-38-2

Credits

A Temple University Faculty Summer Grant, 1990, and a Commonwealth of Pennsylvania Council on the Arts Fellowship in Poetry, 1990, helped provide some of the time during which I composed this work.

The first two poems in this series, "Draft 1: It" and "Draft 2: She" appeared originally in *Temblor* 5 (1987) and then were published in *Tabula Rosa* (Elmwood, CT.: Potes & Poets Press, 1987).

I would like to acknowledge the journals and chapbooks in which these poems were published; in some cases they are revised from their original appearance:

"Of" in *Sulfur* 20 (Fall 1987): 23-27.

"In" in *Mandorla* I, 1 (May 1991): 64-68.

"Gap" in *Conjunctions* 13 (Spring 1989): 40-44.

"Midrush" in *Temblor* 7 (1988): 50-55.

"Me" in *NOTVS* 4,1 (Spring 1989): 39-41; reprinted in *6ix* 1, 1(Spring 1991): 4-6.

"The" and "Page" published as ABACUS 44 (1989); "Page" also appeared in *Conjunctions* 15 (1990): 243-247.

X: Letters was published as a chapbook by Singing Horse Press, 1991. In addition, some of the sections were also published in *Talisman* 4 (Spring 1990): 44; *Aerial*, 6/7 (1991); and *The Women's Review of Books*, VIII, 10-11 (July 1991): 42.

"Schwa" in *Grand Street* (August 1991).

"Diasporas," *Sulfur* 29 (1991).

"Haibun," previously unpublished.

"Conjunctions." A version of this Draft was originally created for the "Poetry and Knowledge" panel (May 4, 1990); St. Mark's Poetry Project, 1990 Symposium "Poetry for the Next Society: Assertions of Power."

Many thanks to the editors who have supported the publication of this work: Robin Becker, Clayton Eshleman, Edward Foster, Peter Ganick, the late Leland Hickman, Bradford Morrow, Gil Ott, Pat and Marla Smith, Rod Smith, Jean Stein, Roberto Tejada, Eliot Weinberger for readings of "X," and the gang of *6ix* (Alicia Askenase, Julia Blumenreich, Valerie Fox, Rina Terry, Heather Thomas, Phyllis Wat).

The minutest details of
    sunlight on a shoe...
had to be scribbled down,
    and with *extension*

        Clark Coolidge
        "A First Reading of *On The Road* and Later"

Feeling this, what should be the form
Which the ungainliness already suggested
Should take?

        Louis Zukofsky
        "Mantis," An Interpretation

Table of Contents

Of

Hinge-loss door, lack latch
ice-ribbed, straws, wad
T-top conglomerate, gritty glass
smash, street-glacier moraine. Pressed
particle board, its jujubes of shellack,
sweet sweet plastic lobbed hither
shredding rips, not too much shelter anyway,
guttering.

Little howling water marbles ice.
Peaked cans junk cubist shingles.
Trounce state cultivated motor auto.
Flop donut. Scat pretzel.
Uneased acceleration and diesel heavy
smoke shot straight rays
at an unseasoned toddler, some unformed
particles strain to come
"eye-shaped." The rest
could care less.
Everything
but weed slack's
loose with melted
writing.
Like one wrote IMPISM right on that rude wall.

Words come just like that, vision.
beak black bleak
cut back through arced site protocol,
member the day. Each micro-face splice gutted,
that
brekkkl they brekk the lyric ruck.

"don't call me a chef honey
I'm a crook"

Skew. Gutter.
A woman scavaged food from that

caesura. Which is
as traditional in this
setting as assigned
places: there's here, and there's there.
A there and a here (meditative
derivative) calls
"I" pivot, middle,
calls "I's" name,
sends "I" winding on site through all that middle
middle space so easily assize:
assimilated viewer of
unfermented ground.

Would you note
the pretty poem
I might (therefore) of wrote?

It's this time-puzzled line-lumber fermenting place,
ice

of words, enormous slant, difficult OF.
Being. Junctures of saturation
beyond catalogue, yet catalogue HAS TO DO
do
syntax; how, why, being beyond me.
In the totality of its unstable relations
unstatable: the what.
This ice is treacherous.

Of is a voice and of is another, and there, here
of,
black and crest, the flair
"of things" in a langdscape.

Thick, this smashed bottle
green
on glaciated street ice, grey octopus.
Thicngs are the
juncted ponts.
Diecast power stick in your craw?
Well, fuck off.

A silent space (I
walk here) populous.
Possessed forsaken bridges, junk
things junked, a hinge from word to word a thingk
of what grammatical conjuncture can seem
adequate to "of"?

Another blizzard on our hands.
Avocado green, almond cream, blue heron, sunbeam
our choice
of colors   our choice of toppings   "rain" down

frozen treats snow pee snow white snow grey snow ice
snow peace   snow gloom. . .

Amazing what a pack of fierceness
binds the backroads between tinker towns and makes
the garrulousness of these travellers virtuously
impenetrable.
We're all
(it seems) troubled by "them's"—
as far as it goes.

Hard to get home; but this is, this travelling
of
is
home.
The streets the malls a homey homeless home
ahung with things.

Micro things and macro things
flip back   "eat this"   "o boy"
in silence chomp your sugary
craw sand.

White snow-chemical for melting
purer than snow
beads the rows like
Hansel's bread. Some trail.
Some house. Some crumbs.
Protest, pivot, empty food-candy,
fatten you up child.
So thirsty
swallow wrong way a cherry
coke. Rub her
cough.
"Red spoil" backs up
the tongue wetting a small mouth'd paper-plastic sip.
Suffocate does it?
Discount!
The little MACS and diet YUMS and PUBS
we know.

Then talk to, about silence

in silence.

Cabin fever
in the grey
world.

Closer? farther?
To study and inhabit
(cars humping up the holding pit)
of, one foot after another, fueled and connected
(lapis and turquoise these are my birthrights)
to something inarticulable:

(rude grey nobs of street junk hinge the rough grey ice)
door after door of
of.

Quarrels, petitions, blanknesses, outrage,
collusions, buy-offs, conjunctions—
with something blown up
it is already here
the debris'

swift
exchange.

This gridlock of possessives
occupies the place
once held by distance.

February-July 1987; May 1991

In

Walks thru the daily
to write the dead

of living
in

every day, chopping
every day a changing, enlarge and isolate, o.

Herein
to dangle small specks over the cribside
surds   harmonics   dang odd
ratios   fishing an
anarchist page.

Oaten paper like bread,
ink of the living waves,
light billows in the grain,

Scritte. *scribe* . crotty
invents
fine fast lines and thick in-
ky turnings

fingerthin mountains
scroll
down to the narrow plain,
a pretty pass.

Creamy cup of tea
cool moon night
neighbor window light.
Unrolls accelerating
streaming

into the kine and pith
of basis.

How white "all color" the color
of luminous death
whose light

San Francisco   Provence   Paestum

is the color of my vivisection
in the world. The world!
the wheaty, milky world.

Whose years?
and what beg-
innings
articulate a blank blanked space, a dotted dotty line?

Just here. . . a draft, a stroke, a kind of fear.

The composted grids, earth lines
where
this hand shakes.
Late summer carnation pods dessicate in
spiky columns, blue grey green, each line is an
inter; there is no action, it is an inter,
(although it was genius to isolate
one action
and make it larger)
there is no story or poem
in.

Every day a little sweeping back, a little digging
out
in
a change

enlarging or diminishing can change.
Depends.

Inside the paper of the page
the iris watermark I suck.
A pen, a hand, an inching haibun,
riddle and edges:
tinted flings of ink wherein
inflection singing
bends time's
minute sounds.

In the backward and forward are
lower and higher
drawn out, drawn on, drawn in

a fine tip pen   a brush flick of
shimmer

amid which nuzzle worms and shaking dew.

Open eye buttabee.
Why the air so blue my honeyo?
Why incredulous by any change?
bud bud bud but bud bud
have turned (should some poem hesitate?)
lactate cherry words
milky spring
IN
to hunger of incipience, perpetual.

So one is finally of it and the "parts" and configuration are
no longer accessible. **Stars imperturbabilty
or matter's inside** Are dark. The mark is dark, the page
dark
is the first imagination of this drawing, this drafting,
these draughts. **Skims of language**

scatter platters of plenty. Patterns
that hunger. **A barque of silage through the sky is** as layers of
translucence, transparencies
on which words could be **feeding**
the cow

        inside the ruminant middle.
read through the other, not so much over but the
simultaneous conflictual overloaded presences for which even
"palimpsest" is too structured a docket. Three dimensional
page, a page place or plage, a plage space, a play splice
the flimsy drops of scrim through which they filter, shapes
and lights
     I make the gesture
        comes through me
A perfectly calm practice **it is this**
yet there is the tension of making a strange train. The run thru the
bi-lingual. Now a very long tunnel totally unexpected. Very dark,
and very long   Entering under the whole structure of
transcendence **Long drawn black**
gold
bold in relation to nature. **fodder strokes**
And now there is no "in" in anything? any
deeper or more intimate **forage**, language
any   knowledge of the   **in** is some effect I
can no longer resist.   **Have no idea what** stop I am.
               grassy drawing on white is
for me to show, to show me it, in. "The green horizon, early
winter dusk" is certainly pretty. I am not getting the force of it, the rebuff,
this constant imperviousness laced with my pleasure.
Implacable

The world. The sorde serif I call myself. Because I am inside,
am a mite in the letter
a traveller thru **are** **the senses of** dark holes tunneling grainy paper.
Gathering all because of being in it,

yet
I am getting the force of it, **in**.

August-December 1987; November 1988; May 1991

Gap

1.

█████ photograph.
A man within a day
of dead

estranged in light, that
flat
flash struck,
half-holds his present

Strange

eyes whitened behind glass
                enamel a "modern" kind of minimal
                mural: indelible black rectangles;
Right on the edge.   who coded the deletions,

lets a child   giving
rip it open

                special numbers, offering a sheet of
                explanations to translate

. . .

"I guess I'll never see you again" I had almost said
                why the deletions had occured.
"little child self"   but I meant "I guess I won't see
folds child soi(e)   it was careful and exacting work
pink silk, tan silk
stroked electricity.   many entirely black pages
                many black squares framed by

                    grids of half-chucked writing
                    had been created
you for a while"
—dried—   by ████████████████
make golden "needles" engaged.

but I had spoken the truth
                    some pages you can't tell anything
hoarded. that aborted opening. one peers at those blackened.

an electric current   trying to read what cannot be read
not to touch
especially
with the "wet hands of tears."   "have been left out of"

2.

                    Black megaliths of memory
Are they too empty or too impacted, protected

Deciphering   "they evoke for me BODY" a dark
shimmer within a square   "activity of repressing
that might be   refabricating of making and
                              losing" if this is memory

a rocking   I have an excellent memory.

of light
is it light? is it leaves? leaven? a place?
a dissolution   opens   a scattering   of the lighter shadows
of shadow   but if it means actually remembering...

within darkness   the darker wall...

Every mark to touch a nerve
in a backwash
of silence   a cicadian roaring   "it is proper to go back

12

of silence: covers and articulates

the bugs crying to each other   to the shadows"

a close packed sound, their
impastos of fluctuating
distance.

The poem's poem   Black pages of gigantic books, tarred
a secret   glutinous with erasure as if
voice muttering porous you   asphalt food were spread
                                        on burlap bread.

sprawled and fragrant

in a webbing of the gaps   Something read that cannot be
woven disclosure. . .   deciphered.

Low late pre-dawn freight
moans, or seems to
"J-w"
as it rushes the grade crossing

its track shining ahead
and away into unfillable

space.

                              I said I had spoken the

On which plot

half wrapped in a sweaty sheet

a sheer drop:

one small point, one of the smallest,
if points had sizes,
yet such, that still
can barely imagine its densities and extensives
if all could be factored and scattered over the breadth
that is

and that
it is.

3.

Someone said this form: but where is it?
    one, start
    two, "the scattering"
    three, a "rush to finish"

even
metal link-
knot's unfathomable
ecliptic

swerving

stars—

Call that point "R" on some
scroll of unrolling:
the there—
that I "was once there"   under a black square
all right   cannot be read or found

and in what language of uneasy rapture.

Grass stars, tree stars, dog stars
misty labyrinth
sores, spots, pocks, fats, jolts
teeming
constellations, and fecund milky spore
of galaxies on darkling sky

or pinked by the city
which dims the stars by local plethoras of light:

There,   with

little swinging words   knots
bits   bugs
bite or shine

little guttering words...

August-September 1988

15

Midrush

Works
thru the dead   to circle

the living flood—

flung expectations
and came to meet the cowering
pairs
in a tarred ark.

lit wreathes,
wassail
doors and houses
edged in blinking.

No one
could give particulars
enough
play, enough force
for what
claims

circles, pustules, chick-thick
baby pox, MD sez boring
disease with flex enough to
twang a sour lyre
"of days";

circle garden overlooked
dying deeper down, flat
even, from the last com-
promises
"of green";

pairing the letters
underneath
siting   citing
the writing under writing.

When the living began
to "labor" (as S. wrote,
rushed) "to die"

10 years work
10 years walk

foot fell into lemony simples
my heart at once in glee and grey
Bar David's star and Marry holly pricks
a day, all day, alway
had, has had had
unseasonable rip-tides
and easily washed away
the flexing thorns and toss amid which we;
shattered the nest to scree,

whereupon whatever thrifty
pots and bits, little
stuff, special mug,
had to be set rite, had to be
set. Assume it.
To paddle dog-wise
in a covenant of breaking—
I tell you!
Like always working against time.

Some flatten the paper
for next year.
Ark opened, the paired
zoo aired and marched.
The colors had been beautiful.
And we have gained more objects
whose provenance is tombs: lavish
pristine colors of the acrid lock.

Swirling marks and snags
low tidy times settle
clays, the pull sedentary.
Yet who will doubt the evidence
silted thru the claim-ragged dirt?

I labor because it was never
spoken and too much, or don't know
much. Or how.

Wraithes of poets, Oppen and oddly
Zukofsky
renew their open engagement with me
wreathing smoke-veils
my eyescreen tearing their insistent
opaque, startled
writing was speaking here was
saying words but,
befit a shady station,
sere swallowed up within the
mouths speaking
and all the words
dizzy with tears
passed again away.

"Where are they now
        dead people?"
"Nowhere."
        "But where
ARE they?"

Human shards   marked
markers   ash   the foiled
feathers of an eaten bird
maintain at the boundaries
of sense and tact
their dun features,

move
mostly much as did in life,
and away, blown
into the incomparable.

What emptiness
they cup for me
from floods
wherein they home?

"Death is the moment
when

what

has been given
away

must be reclaimed."

A clin-
ical rationalist
once he was dead
tempered his endless explanatory head
in wilds and wells of Hebrew prayer.

Walk thru the living
say the dead
our rustling voices
strain
more westerly words

BLOWN

when we have no more   back hosta pods
fluency   flat, black, glossy
cannot, as it turns   seeds

out
form either fully
intelligible wonder or grief.

layered in the leafy mast,
letter bits, the scattered
tabernacle.

It is they that speak
silt
we weep
silt
the flood-bound
written over and under with their
muddy marks

of writing under the writing.

Some epyllion—
pastoral, reclusive, elegiac: flooded
shards drifted up "forever"
thru the clay.
Always another little something—
a broken saucer flower fleck
unremarkable wedge, except its timing
working itself loose in the rain
thru the mum patch
and impatience
some glittery sharp a-flat the wet wide shade.

The house was built on a dump.

Or midrash—
overlayering stories so,
that calling out the ark, it's
Noah hails and harks
new name and number
for
what stinking fur and tuckered feather-fobs
did clamber forth
disoriented. Cramped. Half-dead.

Two names, four names
everything

paired
with words in secret twin
the dry the flooded
remark the same
thing the done
the continual

or unpaired, odd markèd dabs,
but somehow matched
together in their claims

walk thru the dead
to tell the living.

Dressed as a hunter
a robin
hood in tunic-top
of mother-lavish velvet
she talks swords,
greenling
"what are swords FOR?"
"for cutting people"
like I cut the meat;
to try to hurt."

Rousing myself
to a cultural foray
attend, in Merz-y dote,
a chittering sonata.
Amid the *Europäische*
no sense glissades
repeats
this unmistakable refrain:
"rat-ta-tat-tat
bébé."

I will never survive
all this, narrowing skeptical
at straight arrow and oppositional
both. Where is my place?
The name is no.
Is name twin, double yolk,
no too? Is no plus no
a raggy margined yes?
Is no plus no a triangle

wedge of scribbled clay
worked thru claim-slid mud?
How even is with odd.

I get so homeless
mid-race, mill-race, mis-chance,
mezzo "cambio,"
it's lucky I've a house
grounded in this camouflaged locale.

I'm just trying to make
whatever rushed
arrangements
I can and can't
even hear
long distance

because nearer louder
"mommy don't go mommy don't go"
while I have to

work at understanding even
nominally
crossing out and re-
writing odd scraps
in the little ticket square, of days.

December 1987-January 1988

Me

Thru the sealed lid
"91st St"
wherein
mazed letters rem

was wrote, note, she

tolled sky writing:

and it was wide and it was
black—er—blank
a blue A
byss, ab
cess, am
bush,

em space.

—Sky writing—

White shifts, adjustable streaks, scatter
tracks, twigs fell fallen
slack on the asphalt;
the random drifts and drafts its
ens and ems.

Lucid cool green twi-day (say) a struggle
between different
voices competing   don't use that, meaning
that model   that word   to identify
things that   this   isn't it   isn't my   voice

it?

A saturated brush it streaks and blots
a nursery easel struck
with spatter lines—what

speaks?

"me"—

her memoirs?

The big-mouth
bears came chasing me and made me
dash all dark—
far run of little me—and that started
some me screaming *of*
me, a tuneful tidal wave
of much engulfing light.

Do ray me
far so large.

The lines—of green, of pebbled loose—
a fall and scatter near, there mark their move.

Earth star
moon jelly
wobble in waters which
will sting, or sing
you, will

sing already full of voices—
polyphonous voy-
sizz—scissors that sharp
and flat line salt tide
signs:

many;

the sheer, sere
hunger of sight's all-stung
voy-elle. A voice says
"compete to identify." Worse than
jargon—unintelligible. Mental hunger.
"I can't believe my eating."

An old scribe's hieroglyphic-laden
stomacher on which one

Bright cold wide wet clear
writes feather hemp water pot combinations,
sits, placed my hands in beams of bright

tones, light
scales and sounds, sounding luminous
things:

Spoon face, lamp dot,
bread slice, old plate,
cold cup of creamy tea, the moon. . .

"You get to make a red line
on the door.
And then

God of The Death

just flew over their houses
and left them alone."

Listen! linen air
shrouds me in this baby swaddle

others are kind enough to see me running
as if for first-born and call me "her or me."

Dark wrapt. Enrapt,
the cricket breath of a small ark town,
a perch of stone, of pretty stone
the pretty pretty bird which sings a wet
wassail in morrow's dawn

thru naked bliss of space

lines

blow.

Really, could tell you all about me.

I line my eyes with blue
initiation. A bird-thought sits inside my throat.

Am, em a variable space
switched tracks, or dashing marks
which lie in wait
in every dark and light
that gleaming round or rounds this very spot.

Feather breath, I trill,
but sometimes stuck,
can't speak or spit what thrush I got.
So what, that's it, it's just like that.
Red sea, red sea, it covers me.

Spume ruffs
trace marks
no books
but dots and stripes on arcs;
plan

to withdraw my
candidacy, plan
to declare nothing.

And come, or comes, like the "Broadway 1"
as it X's cross the knotted track and
boardwalk wedging shuttle cars marked "Grand Central":

And so I started putting writing
into my poems
and writing over and writing my poems
over—

grey-cream barley, dainty grain-slit eye—
tunnel-wet graffiti over soot patchouli—
cupped my hands, pink around light

rope spot box track signal,
treadmile walking, or riding, as I rode or write,
some sleep
or no—

and these were the fodder foods I offered them
from saffron rooms of light.

Of streams my eyes my hums their streaking lines
they

were all others, live and dead
others they brought
with them dashed into me—
some "me,"
that is, or
no me.

February-June 1988

The

sentences emerge inside sentences
inked on glass, pressured onto the paper
by hands.   **A monoprint, grainy**

Documentation is attended by a flat black wall
made of ink.
The tiniest point can be marked.

> **dim and brilliant
> points, pinholes, dots
> of "the" like the stars**

Days end, map bits, street locations,
"no continuing city"—
it's small-scale wandering here,
there,   **precision of address. There's
the dog, on the rug, quivering,
her toes atwinkle with the dream,
her falsetto "woof woof" tells
she sees no telling what.**

multiples that cannot (ever)
attach the points there are.

Toy-green plates
to feed the dead
little loaves, little flowers;
the "little" regions of fear
there, which   **A squirrel throws down nuts
cannot even be   to make you go away, out of your yard,
back to your house.**

located, scanned
but evanesce.
Fall over dead
tired child.

"They hit   kick   throw stones
break things
run away   rage."

Sentences under
and over, marked,
as a blocked stage, with
tape for where to stand.

Odd books, broken bindings,
triangle flakes scatter out of the "sketches."
We were just going to talk.

A poem called "The" will always be a failure. It is the, the, the on a backdrop of
enormous emptiness that enraptures; just the sheer drop of it flaring against
"clear sky in the desert" or "over a dark lake"

"Brilliant light brass
gold, with narrow scalloped, dark
margin."
Blueing tied in cheesecloth baglets
rinsed the water indigo.

can you imagine? It's impossible
even to understand the
littlest powder, or scaling, or why
the blueing (the coincidence of the name?
the "blur" "blue" "blew"?) is remembered
so clearly and bright.

What I saw or felt in sleeping who can say.
Ticketed for a "me" reel, flickering over incomprehensible zero space
as sonorous hoots of the freight train tossed and wept.
A sight, a sound, a thirsty mouth, a passing wave
4:32 exactly,
endlessly particular
and intent.

Something written on the side—
of what?
Strange changes of scale, and
Sentences inside
sentences, lines beside lines.

Little precisons: solitaire
in a speeding car.

And here's a pink spot in the sky;
in the telescope like nothing.
Can't understand it, but just look—
a penny in some foreign money.
Mars.   Low.   And near.

It's not a gloss either, in either of the senses of that word. Can't make head or tail of it.

Red and muttering, gnarled
whole thorns,
buds, ants at a picnic, fed like birds from her

thrown, she throws them
crumbs,
and struggles away deep in the
cross-hatched grass blades.

Every
day a chopping
a changing a swinging
back,
the blueing swirls an indigo
translucence.
The ants, the person X across a path.

The narrative of precise alignments cannot ever add up, and to what? How anything ever holds together! And the eye that makes it so. Which it might no longer.

Do "a work with many things at large."
Oil stains on the bread page,
a smell of acid paper and the flakes
snowing from "Un Coup de Dés,"

even the fact of a walk,
one "fact," one walk—

ovoid belly, open throated thrush—
generates multiples that cannot ever be
attached
or arrived at to greet. The monoprint
depicted *a* or *the*
down which the oily ink will pour.

And in that conjunction,
the dark of the moon.

Black coffee—tart, rewarmed, and acrid;
a cool cup of creamy tea;
two inch apart twin mysteries, a small
wedge SW arc, my blink
or blick of quadrant space
one silver blue, one golden red—
two planets very "close" together.
That is, as seen from here.

"Curved submarginal
silver-white spot band
basal silver-colored crescent."

"Below, deep, rich golden-orange
with sooty-colored overscaling."

These distances seem as
nothing
sometimes, and sometimes,
no proportion, without end.
A trestle terror on the dark train—
over what? held by what?

The indigo, dissolving, pools in time.
The planetary conjunction in some "now" now gone.
The paint upon glass,
pressed once into one paper

by one hand.
A bird in the brush; tree life; dog life; star life; my life.
An ant flicks into the sand-hole of its home.

A blunt, baffled, continuous wonder.
The poem boring, repetitive, and dull.

"The work is work, however,
 and one is always in the middle of it.
For that reason, 'creation' is not creation"

but multiples that cannot
situate themselves as one
thing.
They were foreign
and distant when they were
near and violent.

"By now she knew almost nothing, no one,
but she knew the shape of the spoon.
She opened her mouth to be fed."

Day after day
with us the angels
grapple
in pinholes of light

close enough to smell his musk
fainting under the
tented sky;

held my hip down hard and
coming hard

held my hip up and cupping.

All through the night
("Let me go, for day is breaking")
morphine suppositories
in pity, in anger,
to calm
the terminal struggles.

A pinhole
a limpid blur from the light
shimmering through it;

a pinhole,
through which the air's waste particles,
these dust mote floater-thready textures of light
BE, no word for be, the ARE, no word for are, the IS,
no word for is, is not.
A THE.

Needle-thin penpoint pushed into the page
a hole. "I can't believe my dreaming."
Startling color, a notational quality,
the sharp kind, not the rolling kind:
the red, the green, the indigo, the pink

the ways they float intensity without chronicle.

Words from before, words
from after,
they
specified into my blank voice
the. They said this this,
this that, and glut in the wonder
of all such singularity became the work.
Calligraphy, a running script, a scroll, with one quick sketch (a day lily and an onion?)
something small in which everything IS.

For that moment.

"Female has vague, angled row of small gold spots
across violet-brown HW **Traces of polychromy. Moved speechless.**
disk." **Struggle! struggle! with the demands**
Stars
in the black void of a clear
sky   we float   motes   Jupiter luminous, bright Mars
this "here," indigo joy

q.v.

can
just slightly
in that conjuncture
write
something written on the side.
Of "what"?

Even the fact of a walk,
those pinks, the small
incommunicable

ALL

rounding the hill, from
the clay orange, an array
all pink and rose and pink again,
spice pink, moss pink, rose walls purple:

to say, or to fail to say
even *this*
is
was the force of it.

Therefore:
staring into the eyes of the past
that grapple back all night,

34

Angel, angel, what shall we name this place?
Pouring oil down the ladder
bone to bone

plenitude and grief; of wordy words,
of wording words, I am
logy from touching the site.

"Let me go, for day is breaking"
I have forgotten what I am.

Sheens of A, luminosities of THE
crosslights and merging blind me
frozen on the thruway.

We were just
going to talk when I found
the sentence doubled, intercut, garbled out,
implausible, shadowed by its
struggling under sense.
Fought as equals
the attenuated shadows at dusk
the black of trees uncanny in the moon,
their deep inside-illuminated dark,
breath weeping harshly into breath
And doubled wrestling,
whitesmith, blacksmith,
And doppelgänger planets,
one blue, one red,
And in that conjunction
the moon, or no moon.

Silence, silence, silence
all unfinished
no detail selected, no pace
fabricated, no array of controlling disclosures.
This poem is flaw flaw flaw

for tetragrammaton awe
belies its formal tongue.
No worth. No form.

Just are. Or is. The the. A a. And what are
they? "What words they throw
away?"

September 1988-May 1989; June 1991

Page

"Exegi monumentum aere perennius"
Horace, *Odes,* III, xxx

1.   Waste places from the very first.
Grubbed marginal plots,
where daisy aster, hairy petaled, was.
Saw sheaves of stirrers strewn by the loading dock.

Stepped and stepped
up the hill under the gate over the road through the field

into the reaches of some certain dead.
Spent mum
inside their rage

that every day decides it will not heal.
"This has been going on for years now."

Rage, range, some other "r" word, a re- or ru-
some word-hunger rampaging
its repression:

thus barely beginning, world, word, wood
would, as all varieties of clouds' lush chaos

BLEW.

2.   She gave me loose crayonings, just
a few colored marks, and I was
frightened, first
folded my gift up.

"It looks terrible."
There is nerve involvement, codine-sweetened pain,

negative dung. Without value.
In which becomes legible
a vacuum from the plethora of materials

and in this space a birth of enigma
to which one owes one's own enigma.

3. It was snow turning to rain, was soft sleet
sheets,
runnels of grey air, was melting on the asphalt, was nothing
to last?

All the words of light,
light among ancient peoples, navigators,
hidden.

Irretrievable estrangements and
unanswerable despair primed
thick-weave canvases which I stretched here.
It was almost too much, it was almost
smothered.

4. For the canvases already primed with words
were to take more.
And the line-streaked white
wobbled

perennially ready
to hold another streak or counter-score.

Eggshell colorings when cracked
show turquoise bleeds
upon the over-boiled white.

Softly silted S's silver water
silk the misted phosphorescent ground
beyond the river's main meander.

A space for deep wake
(screamed "something wet is chasing me"
or "there are worms in my bed") then
the deep wake, passing.

5.   Dawn white
Sunset green

Muddy turgid dirt-like clouds
rainbow arch, and driving madly toward it

rows of makirs
litanies of dead, and dead too young

sequences
interruptions

"making light do what I want"
"weaving webs and webs of silver"

whose very whiteness may be thought too blank
to "tell the white marks from the black."

Apprenticed to it
tripping, my nose down, one corner of an iris, a stick,

light making me do what it wants
and it wants me to weep.

The luminous sheet, the open space, is living air and bright;
or dead, a waiting white like night.

6. What do you want? Is the poem a pony?
You want it to be "noble"
and "stronger than bronze."

You talk of funerals.
I have put a half-sprig
on a coffin above what once had soon before
a face. But was no more.

The poem immortal? you guarantee?

These page-space presences the
negativity
of written words; "parsley" or "bronze," are
airy

as if they turned beyond dimension
and cast the shadows
of what nameless void, whatever voiceless space collected
behind,
and beyond.

Dangerous their generosity
coupled with that shadowy randomness.

7. I crack the spine
of the book, split its muslin glue,
chip the endpapers in a ragged rip.
Inside, folds
and mats of list
camouflage as lines.

It's hiding its impulse even from itself.
Does it want to speak?
Does it want to weep?

Mist. It's four. Rigid without sleep.
"To know what my motives are. . ."
(unfinished)

8.   Line marks names
wavy registers,
a note with folds on the edge of a used sheet
a note with staples and tape
crumpled paper, pencil smudges half illegible
"isolate flakes" hybrid, subversive, inchoate.

The writing on the open page
the underside of itself
as if the underside made words
and, when the busy ripples on the surface stilled,
one saw that other taking shape:

the abstract rush of untranslated words
the space a presence possessed by other spaces

white trace
blank trance
whisper hold.

9.   Being the thing that light comes round, it comes to know
light.

Black, and black and white;
yes, and no, and yes and no;
being and not:
the flicker over space—rectangle, letter line,
spatter marks, irregular alphabet, rath and late;
a scrape, a set of incisions, a score in air:
for various work
has been done in and over this place

various works or workings, works
by,
of,
different hands

hand-space tracks
trek lines

(a trace of spotted light
gleams around the tricky edge of substance. . .)

February-May 1989

X: Letters

This is the alphabet qwertyuiopae[s]dfghjklzxcvbnm.
The extraordinary thing is that no one has yet
taken the trouble to write it out fully. And what
is a beautiful woman?

> William Carlos Williams,
> *A Novelette* (1932).

Q.

I don't know.

What is "natural"
for letters, bud-feathers,
small bumps clumped along my twig.
"Quarry?"
Not an easy question.

Speechless
between each word: years
shown, shone
as quads, months queue;
lead-based slugs line
quoin wedged, double-tied in their chase
by a printer's master knot.

Spaces—
this very minute. Dazed

quagmire.

Of time.

In fact, stuck.
Woman? Letters?
Struck.
They fell from the chase
astonished,
touched to the quick.

W.

Dear X,

Dear who?

Waking at night
with   what about?
penetrating rain, rain
awash thru the screen
wetting
                                    She had failed
a grid-wire window-net.
Telling
time is it like reading:
                    to tell herself what she wanted.

these silver water particles,
shimmering square bubbles,
extend their gridded meniscuses into a space
where   Hard, even
even the smallest
are, or R   to have the stomach for it.
mystery
dank clouds, dirt path, back pack, dead leaf—
this roving, this woven
red leaf, crumpled wrapper, waste water, weeping wound—

whatever
wedges up an intersect,
weights
this or any temporary X.

E.

In eating, I skim the sticky flats called
"Plenty."   It is a strange site.

Have some! can offer
nice engineering
in pretty packages of crackling;
in quaffs of flavored water
a strange, estranged air.

What is enough?
If I eat for the hungry, there are many.
If I buy the coupon'd food,
I crunch sugar and pee salt.

Everything o so "good" and E-Z

to eat for the dead, for the dying,
to keep them in my belly, fetally, or fecally.

R.

Arrived
So soon!   In the lull then
R
Runs the road down hill.   rain, rain and space, and rain
                         swooning, turgid day

She scrolls, runs after unrolling
                    wet sweet grass in the grips
now it's all downhill, and uphill, too,
it's all uphill,   of
running up river and down river.
Can't remember   this
no matter what.   flooding.

O no matter what, I say.
                    Pigments
So I say,   "R"
because it figures, but hard to figure it,
it's   rubbed, scrubbed, marked and
repressed.   erased.

T.

The tea cup in the soft lamp light
travels its little tea breath and milky waves,
its train of time, sentimentally.

I'm thirsty. And it was a question.
  And something   To which the answer is:
                                    there is no "beauty."

            ties
            tries   it.
            tires

                        I can't get myself
Faced   *the simplest things*
                        make yourself a cup of tea
with the tarballs   *somehow*
                        I have to get thru this I cringe
                        every day I cringe
                        It's like living in a tomb.

46

officials are taking a wait and see
attitude.

Y.

Yet every word is a plot:
so story, a story,
why not tell a story, travelling yare and tidy.

> Two years or whatever
> to the day
> by some coincidence.
> There's mesh netting
> yoked to the cliffs,
>
> because
> unstable rocks

a "yolk-yellow" melon,
a diagram and not a poem
a diagram and not a painting:
no need to "fill in" all the color.   present a danger.

Your irony about a voice lavishly remembering.
Because you can't.

U.

Under these urgent, repetitious refusals
are grids
extending
an inconscionable

breadth.
Can never say enough

     (unspeakable)

brown crust spurt:
sparrow upstart in a bush,

whose eager range-drenched beak
     (peep peep)
thru unguent amber, calls,
and resonates
with undertexts.

Beads of amber,
     (peep)
some contain trapped creepers,
are loosely strung upon undulations of umber.

I.

Lavish but inadequate.
Insufficient.

"I"
inside the fabled site
X ist
X'd out.

       Is it inexcusable
          to write an elegy for "I"?

       "I have nothing to say,
       only to show.

I will not present anything
of value.

But the debris! the refuse!"

O.

                             Overwhelming.
Stuck   They try to tell you
two owls hooting   The feel of dying.
thru and thru
the domèd cupola of night.
                       I lose my breath.
water-mouths
Oak
tassel-flowers   *Weighing my options.*

fall.
So much for fall, for spring,   *I lose my breath*
so much fell, outside in and inside out

                      someone must
And if it falls from the sky
with its ossuary payload,   *stay here.*
its slivers of the invisible,
its X,
malplikarigo (to fall, as of snow, Esperanto)—

the foot, pan, rope, loaf,
and wick of twisted flax
oat toast
        "The orphic hope"
                   for a singing stone
the wane and wax of
other alphabets,

primers
of Adams and of Kings,

their one word
(Xantippe or Xenophon)
stand-ins for narratives of X,

and me at my hieroglyphic   Or for orphic ears, to hear,
Mac, as high   or orphic, orphaned mouths,
toned as a Xerox,   "oh oh"

      A well with clefts, letters as stones.

P.

    Pretty doll plates
    of the dead

    red clay, green glaze
    little pips, gifts.

    I am hungry for the food
    left for the dead.

    But I know I should not eat it.

A.

Always apples
are (R)
first:
red planes, yellow planes,
green squares, the most provocative

modeling   Welcome to Aberdeen.
set and round. Piled on a plate.
Articulated by bunting.   Proud to be American.
Apples, A
premier symbol
on the table—
Au and O and I   No Flag Burners Allowed.
Cu and C, K and Ca—
of elements

A
solid type of art.

S.

Especially sediments of unfinished
stories, eroded stories   she states what she has eaten
                                 says
                                 can scarcely swallow

    "stickers   stamps   bus transfers   postmarks
    clippings   paper textures   phrases   letters"
    voluminous overlays carried by valise
    "a more spindly and papery space"
            Imagine a work
    carries   on
    scissors too, plain paper   transparencies of plastic
sheet over sheet   sheet over sheet, scrim light
and glue   sifting words' densities: that slide
in the suitcase   over the others, network by network,
                            that darken
might fall open, might   blackletter solid, thickletter solid
spill at the Gare du Nord   thru which

words: piled into strata
swirled indicators fallen askew, faulted, syncline
scribble scrabble
overwritten, no one way of
ascertaining   something
            and everything
        is like this, simultaneous,
            readable in some parts and sometimes in
            other parts, or in the same parts, un-

D.

Towers of tires the dead dog was
chained there to guard,
dead bitch skeletal
but still sleek, her beautiful fur,
at the foot of the rubbish heap,
starved.
Long starved.
Her master elsewhere.

The dead are the food
                left for us,
                        but don't be greedy.

The door cut her foot.   *It's as if doors are closing.*

F.

Such newspapers as blow across the field
sucking the trash news against the fence

Antenna Sales and Install
Finance Plan Percent
Ho Maid Bakery Products

The military
flew in to dine
at Mt. Rainier Lodge
by helicopter.
Fine use of equip.
Show how something done.

Five pair, then five more pair,
take more, another color.

In the morning,
          the news

On the train,
          the news

What has
          happened, has been done, was
          forged and fulsome
          in my sullen name.

I am poisoned
          thru my ear.

The players
          poured it there.

G.

          A genre:
                    Ballet blanc:

"The most poetical subject   gauze, tulle,
is the death of a beautiful woman"   gossamer
the floating wedge upside down   golems of passion.
that works by electricity.
                    Swans grouped in a graceful, nervous gaggle.
How about that!
              Je
              ate un autre, all right.
              But if "Elle
              suis un autre"
              it seems to be she
              follows another or copies another.

              Gender

              headlight eyes

              adieu.

       "There's a company where they've gone
       beyond gender.
       If they wear dresses
       everyone wears dresses
       —the men wear dresses."

Yea, I will bud out, butt out, yea I will grow
my own green garb, from my own fat self,
and girlie pink socks, toe hole in the sneaks.
Awash
in jumping
I will catch him and her
I will catch and caught whomever
leaps into my flying arms and legs
and dance.

H.

No more frames—   *My hair, it has come out*
no nothing   *it had to, and the heat,*
more than: X marks, like the "yellow spot" in the retina
"my spirit imbedded in glitter"   *I have to wear a hat*
I need the guide to cross-hatching.   *or a scarf, but the heat, it's*
It's horrible,
it gladdens the heart, everything is happening
Do you have one?   *very hard*
                                            to wear a scarf in the heat.

at the same time.

J.

Plague of the first borns
joy-riding through cocaine.   The J of "jour"
Junk subdued, junk exaggerated: truck backs graffito'd,
wire rolls, stereo sets wiring and micro chips matting   or "journal"
strung out of cars as discards, rainbow wads of wire
by the jerk-offs.   the thinnest shred of paper!
So much for sentences.   So much for painting.

K.

Try Esperanto.
Try some mittel-Europäische cooked-up koiné.
The sign indicating "rough air" what
they no longer call "turbulance,"   too
unsettling
the coincidence to trance
to translate Eng. to Esp. and having
all the whirrs the words come out with initial

K's.
Blow down and powder,
diasporas of letters,
the brown rain of stuff
oak tassel-flowers,
kverkoa kvastoj-floroj,
brown   *I have*
strings of quipu   *no choice.*
spring
rosaries of pollen.

L.

It was lost. Memory lost.
"So much time spent looking down the track."
The el dislodges at 242nd St. terminus
lumbers to 238th.
"Let me out of here!" I remember
late   One day they will cull dictionaries
                                    looking for flowers pressed long
                                    ago by sentimental ladies, hoping
                                    among them
                                    for such seeds as would assist
                                    to restart species.
gestures of leaving.
Hard to know which

                    The scale   the land   the rocks   the riches
                             the places   unspeakable.
                    The whole continent driven over a cliff.

memory lost? memory compressed? a dead letter.

Or it was not lost, milky mist moving through the valley
layering pearl cloud, it
was that "memory" was not only "mine"

so it lacerated in ways akin
to clearcut overlogged landscapes
dotted with foxgloves and even-sheared stumps.
And what I am mourning is not "no memory."

Z.

This letter shored
a book of blackened facts;
it faxed the facts and sent them
to itself,
it turned its very pages black.

Dark water Zee rose up to cover them.

Hardly could it be read, even by holding books
to the light,
so thick with inky figures it meant
zero.

Figure after figure
in a row   z after z
It meant sleep.

Sleep in your villages
of stone, and little towns of styrofoam.

X.

"So what does 1 + 1 equal?"

"One!"

Index to it:

        apples: of Demuth, with bananas of
                 of Vlaminck, saturnine quality of
                 of Cezanne, impossible to "describe"
      attention, kinds of; awe; ambush.
      Blow, the recurrence of
      Cancer, the hungry recurrence of
      See also debris.
      Daisies: of Demuth, with tomatoes of
      Emptiness
      frame
      grids for the
      hunger of
      It, as a shifter, its galaxies,
      and junctures
      kited together like odd fruit and crockery
      in still lives. Apprenticed to the Mastery of Textures.
      Sez Letters! I don't know why
      ex-margins' negativities are so sculptural.
      Nor what multiple factors
      are at issue.
      Nor if Many (if arranged well) equals One.
            the little pot of,
            the oatmeal of,
            the scale of.
      Page, as pink. Or black.
      Quire, one-twentieth of a ream.
      Poem: bare ruined quire.
      Rachel, the pinkish color of a powder.
      Silence.

Triangle leap. Solomon's seal.
Totem memoranda: the
Unutterable is or are
Voluminous.
Woman, as a well-inked
letterpress. Kohl round her eye;
she splots on the page as she falls.
X, it marks the spot. It hits the spot.
And marks taboo, and intersect.

Why, as *why*, spoken by the dead.
And dizzying, dismembered zed.

C.

See the staining color, strange cakey streaks, ochre and ombre
that countersink the flux.

Colors create
shadow, they have dimension, they can scale
horizontal connectives, like clefs.

I feel a lot of changes
going on.

I have no choice.

It is disaster faster
than I'm prepared for.

Crysanthamums violets lobelia orchid
dragons, coral and fire, cobalt, cerulean,
carbon, cardinal, carrot, celadon. These colors are lettered,
heightened in intensity by celestial names.

And in the University Museum, a
Chinese bowl shines, quivers, overglazed; it is slathered with
chicken-schmaltz yellow,
a bowl the sheen of childhood fat.

Curator, did
you cut the child's cord with crystal?

I dreamt of doing CPR
into the contraband rictus of the dead.

V.

Vermilion,   muttering, it was
that the voyage also framed the vulva,
that the day vexed it, vibrant and articulated.
It had black velvet strings drawn tight
bound like the piping around upholstery
knots tied to hold forward or down
aglow astripe!   All seasons. Her lymph gland
                      swollen like a volleyball   "White
                      territory?" not white it has a verdigris
                      black long screen a square of blackened
                      import it
                              has a purple mottle wounded friction
                              has
                                 a white as green as bluish gripping grey
                                 as the skin of a strange valediction.

B.

Black nettles   soft redfold flower
blazes of polychrome
Can I say something to console you   Body leased
while trying (one-handed) to undo
the binary?   yet one's only boundary.

The room is dim   Tenacious tenant
a little tush is raised.   evicted.
Four windows
a full room
a touch half-pulled
the clear emptiness brimming silver light.

       Three robin's eggs,
       blue and unbroken,
       lay in their crisp blue nest.

       Cielito.   My little sky.

       I will be ashes
       blew
       out on the street
       blowing thru the night.

N.

N negative plus N positive   "Needless to say,
equals   no amateur
zero, but it isn't   should ever attempt to excavate
as if nothing   a prehistoric burial mound."
had happened
is it?

M.

"Since, as we have already said,
everything in the experience is in motion,"
No memory   Earth mounds
                                        ruined by road cuts.
How can time be made demonstrable except by its debris?

For X. Of X.
I. M. X.

Coda:

Now, for a metaphor,
it could be a black page
or a white page,
or a radiation treatment of the page so that the words
have fallen out

like hair.

And memory, they say, is the "mother" of the muses.
And mother is the instruction not to speak,
to speak partly, to speak euphemisms,
or mesmerizing euhemerisms, to
speak half-deaf to the undertext, to never notice
wantings,
to swallow mourning
to swallow the burning over and over so
that tubes and lobes are scarred with
stig-matter.

Which in order to set forth
must be scattered
must be shattered
smashed against a wall, a door,
thrown against the inoperable sealed-up exit.

January 1989- May 1990
I. M. E.W.B.
June 19, 1914-May 3, 1990

Schwa

The "unsaid" is a shifting boundary
resisting even itself.
Something, the half-sayable,
goes speechless. Or it can't

and Inbetween

            what is, and
            that it is,

is ə Inside

......an offhand
sound, a howe or swallowed
shallow. Sayable Sign
of the un-.

 . . . .

Not the exotic
that is strange but this *strange* puzzle
coil cup "here" where time goes forward

            floats by
            boundaries

a memory *of half*
sayable   vague,
and textured *what*
......*and that it is*
rose or knit or mother-of-pearl
goes speechless
 marks the child *makes*   letters,

64

a signature graffiti, film stills,
saffron light on a west soffit, *Inside.*
And Inbetween
. . . .
lost objects, a tiny doll
and her SWEE-TOUCH-NEE
tin tea trunk of frills.

. . . .

There was a set of girl hankies, saying Monday, Tuesday,

it

the glimmers over 7 new days.

Wednesday, veiled,
those patches of old ice
swampy around tree roots,
low, soupy grey now
so that a great mist covers what was
dirty embankments,
clouds glowering in the nooks of soft valleys
as I rode or ride
so away I do not recognize the vacuum
. . . .
walls of dreams
. . . .

A Thursday, some small good girl
speechless
twirls her plaid umbrella, Friday,
the details.
Struggle tableau:
squeezer-siphons suction out the mucusy sinuses.
Framed from the outside, the flailing

careens thru schwa time
a darter from the murk of silence.

Are lost. Most.
Things of which.

Old familiars, hook toes in amber.
"as still aware as"
Bits matching or unmatched
"gunish helfin."   Can't helf or heft
can't scarcely help
the looming empty weight of emptied time.
Carry an eviscerated bird.
The rubber chicken of a melted past.
Whose kosher yellow feet cut off
stuff up the vacant cavity.

. . . .

Lunchbox Thermos
shatters slivering into

All little tiny "it's" and "its"; there was
a shifting boundary *that is strange*
Open the drawer *speechless*   Of all the lost things
never reseen
hardly bearable never
recoverable, here is something!
An orange blotter! on which brighten
cough syrup bottle- and bird- profiles
edged with a tiny ruler.
WAMPOLE'S CREO-TERPIN compound,
Conjunctures detailed and lavish, Mott Avenue,
Far Rockaway, some of the ten birds
(nested, pecking, chirping, or in flight)
became, in the four decades interim,
endangered.

Other conjunctures blank. Years
this incredible life in time
"simply" erased.
yet day by day   the bits and crumbs
wiped up *by what invisible vectors*
lost   *not lost; half lost,* and lost.
A random swirling pulse of bronzed leaves
breath of a wind intense and subsiding, so
some *falling* here, some over there......
like Betelgeuse and Rigel, 200 million,
where the light lands
whose faded thread chance calls
the pulse more powerful more bright
its factors more unfathomable
than any thing we know.
And we know nothing.

Yet the blue twisted inner
tinkle of milk poured out the broken Thermos
in which mirror-like glass bits splintered......

                    YET WHAT?
                    Is this

rubble accountable? Half-memories, memories half
empty, schwas of memory,
Things, half Things, Things'

effacement. Shadow somber lesions
slopped and filled by creamy prime, so that
almost, they are drawn back
to the stretched silence of canvas.

. . . .

Made in China,
marked down sweater

now marked down half again
to really cheap:
that I,
whatever that is,
can,
without particular investment in it,
stand in the mall,
drawn and quartered like a heifer
trying this
thing in which filiations
(geopolitical, material, and narrative)
thread, and are stored.
Signs readable, but also embarrassing.
"It's so now."   Just
a Knitting whose rich patterns
shuttled thru dark labyrinths
"punch up your Look."

How many miles
have its bumpy acrylics travelled
to have come thus far,
to Springfield Mall,
adrift from its pence-paid maker......
The weave of its wefters, its shunters, its buyers,
its filmy yarns' dictation and direction

                    Who can
                    must Credit.

And the bright tags and the price codes are tacked in plastic string,
and anchor it

a sound halfway between articulation and disappearance
a sound falling out
or beginning to fall out,
voiced, but seemingly voiceless.

. . . .

Unheard vocalics taken for granted
are making, are mocking up
words, that
no one can put their finger on, yes
abrim with scrambled schwas
and unfathomable glissades.

Just as a febrile distracted
ichneumon bug, the leggy one,
wavers shadowy from corner to corner,
flies panicked, and climbs treadmills of wall,

this loss seems irrevocable.
I quiver in my pinhole time
where bits of voice are buried
in broken, unrecoverable objects,
the flowered butter dish, a-smash
Trip films torn from a stolen camera, and dumped,
bits and turns, the buried sounds of stifled voicing.
And were I to cry that out, who'd want to hear me do it?

> Gap and glut
> "most people"

remains between the two
"unwritten."

And cried out
who would bother to listen
among those frantically fluttering angles?
. . . .

> Bunched up.
> If only.

Thus, travelling hungry, I lost my sense of direction,
with "metamorphosis"
and "petrified human desire"
my dearest companions.

June-November 1990

Diasporas

Thru the rusty furze, thru the misted light,
thru the hungry books
words
related to the torn debris
lightly fall,
brush
the stumbled walker
who enters scenes of scattering by the gate of loss.

Wordlessness whirlwinds words
at that limen, articulating multiples
that cannot even be attached or
arrived at to greet, so foreign and distant, and
so near and constant,
the sets were experienced as one confusion.

These spaces of dispersion
are marked with bourns
which disappear amid the fields of scree
as stones.
So gifts are swallowed up by gifts.
Even erasure is erased.
In this, what residue remains?

The green horizon, winter dusk,
curbs, ground-down dabs,
sleek styrofoam weathered into gritty pebbling,
food pressed face down on the asphalt
scattered
        thru   the   flicker-ridden   labyrinth,

      here

        we are,

gripping frayed ends of the yarn together,
bull-face and seeker.

This small evidence of hope, that our flawed light

MEASURES THE HEADLINES

warily
point for point.

'Twas the new year cold,
and the old year done.
Hung a full moon
twice that 31st.
It rose in the dark,
and it rose at the dawn.

Introducing the "J" of jour, the our of hour,
versus "A": flat, primary, simple.
First it's J.
Then it's A,

parry and grapple, sleek and troubled,
leg over leg on the shimmering tarmac.
Advantage agnostic.

Happens
your yeasty jousters
are oddly,

like Ques. and Ans.,
odic and oracular,
joy and anger,
just evenly matched.

Matted mists rise
from felled leaves
after the whirlwind.
Melted mists
mishegoss and worse,
Names that cannot rise.

Names wedged in cardboard huts from
        major appliances.
                Xeroxing

city by city;
        stacks on automatic feed, little
                rustlings over vents,

mechanisms under glass,
        darkly you thought
                THAT was a what?

an empty carton? THIS simply
        rags, drain-plugs, trash
                rolled up in bags by the Department

of the Treasury, askew
        and stinking. But look:
                what is and that it is.

                On the pivot
                of a vast immired time
                the little fizzle of firecrackers
                went pop-pop in the humid silence,
                the irradiant bleakness
                of this midnight turn. Why it's "already"

1991

one more throb of pops down wicks flung into the distance
                and all around a void of open time
                to the right of us, to the left of us.

And want to rise up, compelled
to change the order of events,   to overturn
                    priorities and registers.   Own up
                    powers dominating an unseen. They
            solid for war: And drag to camp that Trojan
                    Horse,   the surgical
            metaphor.   Of course, modernized,
                    administering anaesthesia highs. But
                    who was the patient "etherized"?
We profiteering, prophesying, sighing.
      The center, an abyss   The A repeated useless over
                        and over   lolling doped
                uh uh uh uh uh uh uh uh uh uh ayh ayh
            turning to I I I I aye aye aye aye ai ai ai ai
scattered by one, one, one   waste pretense. It was the dust rising
            and falling that formed the holden
                        source of all this "dreath."
      It was solid blackness up from the dis(re)membered
                        ordures and ordeals.
It was children once again to be issued bumbled stumps for feet.

            My m-m-ry looked back and turned to salt.
                A glistening dolmen.
                Does it want to weep?

                "It" doesn't choose
                "It," is chosen
                by the frozen one-way track
                of time

                Implacable

                    (Light!
                "opening" birds
                "lofting, spinning"
                transcendent flocks
            flecking the wide "horizon"—signs

of a poet,
or for one.

Why not car roof snow slid soft,
and refroze drip-marked over the windshield?

Why not furtive copies, ripping off
the part-time joblet,

with one long hair
fallen onto the glass screen, recurring
on all her Xeroxes, twisting at random,
circling words.

Dingedicht, Dongedacht, Dingedicht, Dongedacht)

And into the valley of death
I or J wrestled
pulled apart at the jointure or juncture.
The little rocks and bumps
were welded together with blood, and blood
filled the streams, which were called "runs," and
misty blood evaporated in the hollows.
Such a tiny set of hedgerows over which the soldiers fling
and were flung.
Cost it out.
The deep hung crevasses of shape and meaning
make
just a flicker over ever-whispering space.

"Then" I felt the dead, returned as deer, sidle
silently in the night to the block of white,
rub and lick

mutter in the various
clotted tones of
their living voices

one word:
>   creole of creoles.
>   The rest blown away

>   Into the incomparable.

>   Struggling with

Unfed. Thug.   Bread.   ashes wet
Flagged pilings. Blood maimed.   ashen face
Flayed pages. Manna and matter   in the drear station

>   and historical dread.

So that the first digits of my MAC card are exactly the number of
civilians killed at Mylai or Mylae, alongside the final digit, which
is the number of persons in my family, allowing, or not, for the
ambiguities of reporting, lies, cover-ups, disinformation,
disingenuous spokespersons—so often now women—, and who
or what one is counting; also whether one numbers the dead
and the living, or only the dead, or only the living, on either the
"historical plane" or the "personal." Or only numbs the living.
So that there is an enormous amount of webbing and one is
taxed with the question what to do first or at all: unwrap it as
from the mummy, sort it and maybe the little ants can still be
persuaded to help, follow its loose-leaf strands as they
blow thru the arena, neaten it, perhaps by a traditional weaving,
brush it away like gossamer spinning, hang it all, or some
unknown and awkward correlation of jerky, improvident,
undeveloped, and spastic gestures, neurological overflow in
which scryers find a symptom of ("unliterary") disorders, giving
unintended and/or unreadable consequences. So that—

>   "It means

>   seize hold of a memory

76

as it flashes up

at a moment of danger."

hole of a memory

Get real!

June 1990-June 1991

Haibun

Drinking Lethe-eau from one spring
Mnemonsyne-water from another,

like wine and coffee, opposite greeds
alter the micro balances in the banlieus.
Up and down, up and down
or open and taut, open and taut,
the sand pendulum pattern of Lissajous figures
makes a *here* always
slightly off-center from the last stroke.

It is unseasonably warm here and the leaves stayed on the trees
for the longest time—even stayed green—for a long langorous
autumn, almost a case of arrested development.

Then talk to about silence, in silence.

> A glass of water, a slice
> lemon.
> Golden mountains, silver moon.

At every moment, there are oddities of the journey.

Thursday: found great offense.
Sunday: fountains withdrew.

> Dark and somber dreams of walking,
> low song clouds
> in unbecoming places.

●

"Ever notice tiny specks or strings darting in and out of your eyes? The Mayo Clinic Health Letter says that although these semi-transparent bodies, called 'vitreous floaters' are annoying, they don't affect vision."

> Reassuring.
> Convenience store
> dead air, Flav-R-Pac
> salts it.

The trip, the treck, the record, the haibun-ordinary details: a high wind, 11:50, blew all the papers off the table when American haiku extruded from the texture

> walking
> thinking
> bitterroot
> beebalm.

Three blanks, beginning middle and end
Two blanks, thesis and antithesis
Thirst in every direction.
But one learns not to watch
the stately randomness of unaccountable figures.

●

I wear some clothes of the dead, and eat some of the food left in their cupboards, Vermont maple syrup talismanic, a soft summer nightgown, use a hanky with an "E." The clothes survive, and float up onto this shore rather than some other, some sour thrift shop rummage sale,
and buying I've had fine linen handkerchiefs, with initials "WTN" random finds
some dead man's debris
living on after him.

And there are many clothes strewn in the street
Where I walk to work
A pink polyester sweater.

Where?
at close range.

●

The street man pushed his doctored shopping cart ahung with
stuffed and puckered Hefty bags. Dangles from the front, one
plastic wink, a bubble "California Raisin."

And the starling, junk bird, slammed into the brick wall during
the storm? Stiff and dead. Cartoon dead, feet out, x's for eyes.
And the grey dog exploded on impact on I-95?

Glisten of bright glass bits. Buffer sofa in the waste spaces, the
many dulls of brown, brush twist total. Denial and remaking.
The little squibs unseen that float thru on the side, travelling out
of the frame. Here, the first 200 patriotic customers will receive
FREE American flags.

I should use the pentamenteur line, and organize things better.

●

Experience what the locals already know. Networks of
reminiscences in the reading, constructions of déjà vu, lush chaos

transparencies of the scattering—it is so blown away that it
appears hardly at all, even the residue is invisible, hardly a trace.

So there is no pure art, just something sliding over the site
between the illusion of realism and despair, grappling for a
foothold or handhold, every

mark
is made in time, time that is not spent almost weeping
and work work work
like 7 dwarves
all for the moment
of falling away.

Transparencies and opacities slide across each other, pick out
each others' figures and grounds. Words are there, also shaded
drawings, muted myopias, floating smudges of mist, brown
spores fine and invisible as dust shot off by a little fungus called
the earth star. And crossed sticks.

Widen what's wide.
Narrow what's narrow.
Don't bring it to the middle, intensify its reasons.
Some things, when ripped,
need to be ripped more.

●

At 10th and Montgomery, the glass smash where I walk
to work, the recurrences of dreck, where I crackle the debris
step by step, a sparrow tried to fly up to a linden grappling a
doughy crescent of pizza in its beak. Which it had to drop,
the choke of crust too heavy

       An octave above
       what chord?

be asking why I am here, why here, why this, why these bonds,
why this matter, these little bits of matter *me* and *it*, and

       "the void-strewn firmament"

in which the biggest statue of a Holstein
here to be seen

rises on a bluff over New Salem, North Dakota,
look left,
I-94 travelling west.

●

Being polygeneric, why did all your work behave as elegy?

The landscape bare, without
consideration, without qualities.

"Who are you?"
"I am nomad."

The arking reach of sky, the starry bliss, dew of light, prolix,
unimaginable but present, in which the traveller wrestles with
flashing visitations of vector

Quick rumpuses of solidity
Intercept the endlessly porous.

The Milky Way is "ours" and even we are to the side of it.
And every cell flies up and cries *hark arc*. And "me" a little
blown dust weed seed
whistling, so does it matter if it rise or fall? silvery fibers afloat or
sodden?
No matter how, which way, or why
we drown in the aura of our own joy.

●

One can see why, though, the myth spoke of a Call, "your name
here," sounded by a Them or The from cruxes
of silent bowl-shaped spaces:

Something definite, so to speak.

Twinkling planets
night trees net,
the fireflies drift, the stars float
as green-bright meetings just above our breath.

There are marks and markers even in the flattest waste places.
On my driveway. Stunned by a few twigs, a dead beech leaf,
some crumbling asphalt shadowy in the streetlight. Whose
name did they call? I answered *here am I.*

But who are they? And make a small mark and then, blessedly
(though sometimes the "I" is unrepentent, annoyed),
it
is swallowed into the void.

●

June-July 1991

Conjunctions

> "Conjunctions have made themselves
> live by their work."
>> Gertrude Stein, *"Poetry and Grammar"*

1. To write with the formidable consciousness of loss *thus:*

repeatedly emphasized under cross-examination: skin, sky, fog,
    silence, and
humility.

To vow to write *so that*
if, in some aftermath, a few shard words,
chancily rendered, the potchkered scrap of the human
speck
washed up out of the torn debris, to write
so that
if your shard emerged from the shard pile

people would cry, *and* cry aloud "look! look!"

If yours were the only poem,
the only fragment
left, those who came after,

part of a running script on the running subject
"on the whole unbounded *and* contingent" it
was a truly temporal predicament.
"We seem to behold only a small part

of an infinitely extended structure."

2. "Unconscious in a pool of blood
on the white linoleum floor."

Assailed kosher products, racial intermarriage, the immigrants
just coming in. Bamboo writing, juxtaposition, *and* typographical
irregularity.

Closed circuit at Market East—the flicker
"Supreme Court today"
the dissolve
"create the corporate environment" *and*
tonight's TV, "Number One
with a Bullet."
"Horror & violence do not exceed moderate levels."
You know what I'm doing.

3. Inside the small space I can hardly name
small time jog around the track
6 laps, one *and* one-half miles—
no more sheer opulance—
6 dusky runners, me *and* mine
the miles.

The way that can be named is not the way.
But will you take a way that has no name

catch up with
forgiveness?

4. Call this poetics "posthumous."

The articulation of previous silences,
the invention of memory, *and, and but*
the hole, again I said hold,
I have in my head,

yeasty,
a soft brown low scum bubbling
with the tide. *Yet, or nor*
sound be always there,
if you had ears to hear, *or* eyes, *or*
borrow them to burrow here.

A sheet with centers of letters
burnt out? black pages? blanks?
scraps of tongue in combinatoire?
what is "a normal book"?
"Don't laugh; it's paid for."

The social world, they said, "drained from his work"
and didn't say "more's the pity."
Snippets of dialogue?
Syntax torqued?
Stuff roped together on a weekday?
Winking rays that scatter?
Speak from the site
as if you were already dead.

5.   One bronze tea leaf had stuck to the side
away from the milky sweet.
And, nevertheless, I tip the cup; I rinse it in.

"Can this watch be fixed? It's very good
and very old." Holds it out, gold
to me, the living limen beyond which
she lies.
Shattered, babbling, she
wonders if her old watch
can be fixed.
A deathbed.
Still, I can see why it's in her head.

6. Hit the buzzer. Call time.
No one wants mere political correctness, *but*

"I keep trying to imagine the
post-structuralist woman in a supermarket."
I can imagine little else.

The eye-door swings open for me *and* my cart.
Blink rate, you're really on your own now!

7. These pinholes we live
in, the little
songs we sing
stars; twinkling,

so the restless perversities of letters can shimmer
on a lenticular plastic surface.
One thing looks like it's fighting *or* biting the other,
swallowing, tumbling, pecking, *and* electric with pleasure,
the whole poem at each other's throats.

8. *But* we seem to hold only
a small *and* inchoate part
spread so veiled *yet, or and* fecund,
lavish with daylilies.
Lavender. Orange. Peach. Creamy pink *and* bright.
Maroon, this with Yellow center *and* at the core
a Green eye.
Ribbed, curled, cupped, stippled
and even fragrant, lemony.

One-day wonders
in whose corolla sometimes
alight spicebush swallowtail;
one goddess of beauty

splashing pollen,
the lily her shell.

Or silver streak of neon on a muggy night.
It's that poetry
has had brightness, such positive brightness.
It was luminous, *and, or rather or* forgiving,
light pulsing with shadows under the trees.

Time is sizeless.
But, likewise then
someone puts the spoon to our mouths.
We moue *and* juice *and* gum *and* chew.
Something mortal,
stuffed like a brico plug into infinity.
Like any half-done job with half-assed tools
it'll never fix it.
Sooner *or* later the plug falls out
and here

coincides with nowhere.

"To write is to discover this point."

9. Dawn, line, quirk, orthography, abyss.
Pretend it is all margin.

The border, the letters, as the page, are white.
It was all luminous *and/or* all destroyed.

Then we will understand *neither*
these arrangements, the small scraps disbursed

nor the act of documenting:
"I'm on record as...."

And not understanding, we will join
them in fear;

fear, which, with joy,
is the fact of substance.

10. Go there, go there, go down its numb stair
down the one-way ice-cold track,
steel-folded pilgrim.
Walk shiva.
Stone, pause,   margins,
Snow lightly falling freezes your amazement.
Trek dumb
into your number
so you will always remember
in the Gedank-
mal
hall

they gave you,
traveller.

11. I walk, *also, or because* through ordinary objects: tomato
paste, soup spoons; zoo trip permission forms; a monthly
trail-pass in a clip-on holder. Master of the Female Half-Lengths. I
walk to *and* fro, around the island. On which a black *and* white
potholder with a cowface. On which three raw chicken legs, fat
and skin to skim *and* pull away. On which a pencil, a lite brite,
some dregs, wedges, crumbs, chockablocks, *and* arrears. Facts
in a site of several important dimensions. No describing the way
it, they does sway.
An octave below what lowest chord, in what terminus for music
lies this rumble?
I wish I were a pair of supremicist red squares.

12. We aim for linkage at 100%, we accept
at a much lower percentage.
Here it is already the debris, animal cuts, paper products,
the float of smaller rectangular
colors called "them" *and* the red one called "that."

The coupage from these mottled views
can they be donné?

The given? scarce are these words out when
Ferocities of morning unhinge ennuis of night.

To move one foot after another,
to articulate the bread page,
to wave harbingers onto the construction site,
to squeeze the pulp *and*   pat it on the deckle
are the works.

13. Not the exotic
that is strange *but*
the small

puzzle coil cup where time goes forward
and we try to feel what has happened
and not just to ourselves
and bits of memory float up
vague *and* random compensation.
A kind of scrying after all.

People put down what they saw *or* felt like, there were days
designated. Questions. Lee way. "A fleshy material identity."

It was "anthropology-at-home."

"Some use of one of the harsher sexually-derived
words may be heard."

Maps *and* to-scale projections on the desk.
The normal detritus of normal everyday consultants
a-weep over this time
and not just because it is time
and they will die in it.

People were spotters.
Sometimes they recorded their acts;
doing, seeing, "crossing, struggling, naming,"
"watching doubting wheeling shining *and* pondering,"
and still, and/or yet they were called
"a recording instrument of the facts."

"three weeks old. Permanent brain damage."

"Pair deny charges of case-fixing."

"Let them eat crack."

Were sometimes asked to write
on certain categories of behavior such as
"the relation of superiors to subordinates,
and subordinates to superiors."

14. What, then, is the size of the loss?
The size is a triumph.
A chemical glue drying askew
bares the device.
It is called "anguage."
It won't be the same, ever where
or far away since.

So what is the foggiest notion
you say you don't have?

Anarchist *and*   pleasuring
a flowered surface
a surwind on the flood of the sea
splintered bountiful marks.

I throw it all as far as I can,
and it blows back, blows black,

"a certainty based on the acceptance of doubt"
in "texts at once perfect *and* incomplete."

April 1990-July 1991

Notes

Draft 5. Notes to "Gap." The deleted pages are from FBI files.
"The little child self" from Mallarmé's *The Tomb of Anatole*,
specifically Paul Auster's translation. "An Activity..." is Regina
Schwartz explaining interpretation; the notion of memory as
interpretation recently in Mary Jacobus. "It is proper" from
Irigaray. The black books are by Anselm Kiefer. "Someone" is
the dancer Sharon Friedler; "the form" occurs in Japanese
music: "jo"—introduction; "ha"—the scattering; "kyu"—the rush
to finish.

Draft 6. Notes to "Midrush." The citation "Death is the
moment..." from Annette B. Weiner, "Stability in Banana Leaves:
Colonization and Women in Kiriwina, Trobriand Islands," in
eds. Mona Etienne and Eleanor Leacock, *Women and
Colonization: Anthropological Perspectives*, 287. "Rat-ta-tat-tat
bébé." from Kurt Schwitters, UR-SONATA, 1923.

Draft 7. Notes to "Me." Someone said Emily Dickinson used the
term "sky writing" in *Letters* I, 81-82. An image of Remedios
Varo's painting "Harmony" (1956) enters into one section.

Draft 8. Notes to "The." "No continuing city," Hebrews 13:14.
Description of "fours" from a day care center. Butterfly
descriptions from *The Audubon Society Field Guide to North
American Butterflies*, 819, 787, 795. "The work is work,
however..." from James Scully's essay "Line Break," in *Line
Break: Poetry as Social Practice*. Jacob, in Genesis 32: 24-32.
"What words..." from Margaret Holley on Marianne Moore.

Draft 9. Notes to "Page." Horace, *Odes*. "I have constructed a
monument more permanent than bronze and loftier than the
noble Pyramids—a monument which no squalling rain, no
gale-force wind can ever undermine.... In fact, I shall not totally
die: a good chunk of me is going to elude funeral parlours." (My

modification of a Penguin translation of III, xxx) "Making light" and "weaving webs" are H.D. on film; "tell the white marks" is Williams on Marianne Moore, and "isolate flakes" alters *Spring and All*.

Draft X. Notes to "Letters." "I have nothing to say...": modified from Walter Benjamin. "Orphic hope..." Barbara Johnson. "Stickers, stamps..." Kurt Schwitters, or something about him. "More spindly..." Robert Hughes, *Time* (December 26, 1988). "The most poetical subject..." by E. A. Poe. "Je" etc., Arthur Rimbaud. "There is a company..." Beverly Blossom. "My spirit..." Robert Stepto. "Since we have already said..." Susan Horton. Gained tread on the smashing from Bradford Morrow's citing Dowell Coleman: "That compact little glass, a small wine glass—but broken it seemed to contain enough glass to make three, or four, that size."

Edmond Jabès (Rosmarie Waldrop, trans. *The Book of Shares*): "The readable is perhaps only the unreadable smashed to pieces."

Draft 11. Notes to "Schwa." "The unsaid," M.M. Bakhtin, "Methodology for the Human Sciences." "Metamorphosis" and "petrified human desire" from Marianne Shapiro, *Hieroglyph of Time*. The line "Wer, wenn ich schrie," translated severally from Rilke, *Duino Elegies*, I.

Draft 12. Notes to "Diasporas." "Creole of creoles," a phrase by Rei Terada. The end citation from Walter Benjamin.

Draft 13. Notes to "Haibun." "Lethe" through "water...": modified from Leonard Kress, citing Pausanias. Lissajous figures: Philadelphia's Franklin Institute. Mayo Clinic letter cited by Marc Schogol in the Philadelphia *Inquirer*. "First patriotic": Sears ad. "Void-strewn": Blanchot on Mallarmé in *The Siren's Song: Selected Essays*, (Bloomington: Indiana University Press, 1982).

Draft 14.   Notes to "Conjunctions." There are citations from the Philadelphia *Inquirer*, Metro section, Friday, April 6, 1990. There are citations from the Classification and Rating Administration (CARA) criteria for films. From an article by Meyer Shapiro, and an article by Paul de Man. The "social drained from his work" is a *New York Times* review (Sept. 8, 1989) of the photographs of Aaron Siskind.

"This point at which we see time as sizeless, involves us in infinity and is the point where 'here' coincides with 'nowhere.' To write is to discover this point." Blanchot, *The Sirens' Song*, 119.

Materials on Mass Observation, are, inter alia, from Humphrey Jennings and Charles Madge, "Poetic Description and Mass-Observation," *New Verse* 24 (Feb-March 1937); especially from David Chaney and Michael Pickering, "Authorship in Documentary: Sociology as an Art Form in Mass Observation," in *Documentary and the Mass Media*, ed. John Corner (London: Edward Arnold, 1986). Also Diana Collecott, "H.D. and Mass Observation," *Line* 13 (1989); it is from this article that I first learned about Mass Observation.

"Fleshy"—Linda Alcoff, article in *Signs*. "Crossing, struggling, naming" is Geoffrey Hartman on Roland Barthes' analysis of Jacob and the Angel, in *Midrash and Literature*, ed. Geoffrey H. Hartman and Sanford Budick (New Haven: Yale University Press,1986). "Watching doubting (etc.)" is Mallarmè's "Un Coup de Dés," as cited by Blanchot, *The Sirens' Song*, 245. "The size of the loss," Clayton Eshleman on exploration in poetry, *Conductors of the Pit* (New York: Paragon House, 1988), 5. "A certainty..." John Berger, on Picasso. Final words from Renée Block, "Midrash," in ed. Callaway & Greene, *Approaches to Ancient Judaism*.

Rachel Blau DuPlessis, Professor of English at Temple University, is the author of *Writing Beyond the Ending: Narrative Strategies of Twentieth Century Women Writers* (1985), *H.D.: The Career of that Struggle* (1986), both from Indiana, and *The Pink Guitar: Writing as Feminist Practice* (Routledge, 1990). Her poetry is collected in *Wells* (Montemora, 1980), *Tabula Rosa* (Potes & Poets, 1987), *Draft X: Letters* (Singing Horse Press, 1991), and a book of long poems, *Drafts (3-14)* (Potes & Poets, 1991). She is the editor of *The Selected Letters of George Oppen* (Duke University Press, 1990), and, with co-editor Susan Friedman, of *Signets: Reading H.D.* (University of Wisconsin Press, 1990). In 1990, she was awarded a Pennsylvania Council on the Arts grant for poetry.

photo by Ron Tarver

99

Potes & Poets Press, Inc.
181 Edgemont Avenue
Elmwood, CT 06110

POTES AND POETS PRESS PUBLICATIONS

Mickal And, Book 7, *Samsara Congeries*
Bruce Andrews, *Excommunicate*
Bruce Andrews, *Executive Summary*
Bruce Andrews, *from Shut Up*
Todd Baron, *Dark as a hat*
Dennis Barone, *The World / The Possibility*
Dennis Barone, *Forms / Froms*
Dennis Barone, *The Book of discoveries*
Lee Bartlett, *Red Scare*
Beau Beausoleil, *in case / this way two things fall*
Martine Bellen, *Places People Dare Not Enter*
Steve Benson, *Reverse Order*
Steve Benson, *Two Works Based on Performance*
Brita Bergland, *form is bidden*
Charles Bernstein, *Amblyopia*
Charles Bernstein, *Conversation with Henry Hills*
Julia Blumenreich, *Parallelism*
Paul Buck, *No Title*
John Byrum, *Cells*
O. Cadiot / C. Bernstein, *Red, Green & Black*
Abigail Child, *A Motive for Mayhem*
A. Clarke / R. Sheppard, eds., *Floating Capital*
Norman Cole, *Metamorphopsia*
Clark Coolidge, *The Symphony*
Cid Corman, *Essay on Poetry*
Cid Corman, *Root Song*
Beverly Dahlen, *A Reading (11-17)*
Tina Darragh, *a(gain)2st the odds*
Tina Darragh, *Exposed Faces*
Alan Davies, *a an av es*
Alan Davies, *Mnemonotechnics*
Alan Davies, *Riot Now*
Jean Day, *From No Springs Trail*
Ray DiPalma, *The Jukebox of Memnon*
Ray DiPalma, *New Poems*
Ray DiPalma, *14 Poems from Metropolitan Corridor*
Rachel Blau DuPlessis, *Drafts #8 and #9*
Rachel Blau DuPlessis, *Drafts 3-14*
Rachel Blau DuPlessis, *Tabula Rosa*
Johanna Drucker, *from Bookscape*
Theodore Enslin, *Case Book*
Theodore Enslin, *Meditations on Varied Grounds*
Theodore Enslin, *September's Bonfire*
Norman Fischer, *The Devices*
Steven Forth, *Calls This*
Kathleen Fraser, *Giotto : Arena*
Peter Ganick, *Met Honest Stanzas*